9/05

LIVING WELL
GOOD
MENTAL HEALTH

by Shirley Wimbish Gray

THE CHILD'S WORLD®
CHANHASSEN, MINNESOTA

The
Child's
World

Published in the United States of America by The Child's World®
P.O. Box 326, Chanhassen, MN 55317-0326
800-599-READ
www.childsworld.com

Subject adviser:
Diana Ruschhaupt,
Director of Programs,
Ruth Lilly Health
Education Center,
Indianapolis,
Indianapolis

Photo Credits: Cover: Stockbyte/Creatas; Ariel Skelley/Corbis: 15, 24, 25; Bernard Bisson/Corbis Sygma: 9; Charles Gupton/Corbis: 14 right, 27; Corbis: 6 (Howard Sochurek), 11, 23 (Annie Griffiths Belt), 25 right (Paul Barton), 29 (Steve Raymer), 31 (Tom & Dee Ann McCarthy); Custom Medical Stock Photo: 7; Duomo/Corbis: 5, 12; Jeff Greenberg/PhotoEdit: 16, 18; Myrleen Ferguson Cate/PhotoEdit: 19, 26; PhotoEdit: 8 (David Young-Wolff), 10 (Michael Newman), 13 (Mary Kate Denny), 17 (Robert Brenner), 20 (Spencer Grant), 21 (Richard Hutchings), 21-right (Felicia Martinez); Tony Freeman/PhotoEdit: 10 right, 14; U. S. Department of Agriculture: 22.

The Child's World®: Mary Berendes, Publishing Director

Editorial Directions, Inc.: E. Russell Primm, Editorial Director; Elizabeth K. Martin, Line Editor; Katie Marsico, Assistant Editor; Olivia Nellums, Editorial Assistant; Susan Hindman, Copy Editor; Sarah E. De Capua, Proofreader; Peter Garnham and Chris Simms, Fact Checkers; Tim Griffin/IndexServ, Indexer; Elizabeth K. Martin and Matthew Messbarger, Photo Researchers and Selectors

Library of Congress Cataloging-in-Publication Data
Gray, Shirley W.
  Good mental health / by Shirley Wimbish Gray.
     p. cm. — (Living well)
Includes index.
Contents: Take a deep breath!—Your brain—Does worrying help?—Too much stress!—Good mental health!
  ISBN 1-59296-082-0 (lib. bdg. : alk. paper)
  1. Mental health—Juvenile literature. 2. Emotions—Juvenile literature. 3. Child mental health—Juvenile literature. [1. Mental health. 2. Emotions. 3. Anxiety. 4. Stress (Psychology)] I. Title. II. Series: Living well (Child's World (Firm)
  RA790.G817 2004
  616.89—dc21   2003006280

TABLE OF CONTENTS

CHAPTER ONE

4 Take a Deep Breath!

CHAPTER TWO

6 What Does the Brain Do?

CHAPTER THREE

10 Does Worrying Help?

CHAPTER FOUR

14 What Is Stress?

CHAPTER FIVE

19 How Can You Develop Good Mental Health?

28 Glossary

28 Questions and Answers about Mental Health

29 Did You Know?

30 How to Learn More about Mental Health

32 Index

TAKE A DEEP BREATH!

"Come on, Dad. I don't want to be late. It's time to leave for the game," Alex said as he ran down the steps. "Let's go!"

"Relax," his father said. "You have plenty of time before the basketball game."

Alex could not relax. His stomach felt like it had butterflies in it. His hands were sweating. All he could think about was basketball. This was the final game of the season. Would his team win? Would he score any points?

Finally, Alex and his father got to the gym. Alex took several deep breaths and then ran over to join his team. He felt better as soon as he started warming up. "This is going to be fun!" he thought.

Have you ever felt the way Alex did? Maybe it was before your soccer game. Or maybe it was before a spelling test. Most children feel excited or nervous before a big event.

Your brain is in charge of the butterflies in your stomach. In fact, your brain is in charge of all the emotions (ee-MO-shuns), or feelings, that you have. Learning how to handle your feelings is part of good **mental** health. Then you can have fun and do your best, just like Alex did.

Alex was able to handle his worries about the game so he could play his best.

CHAPTER TWO

WHAT DOES THE BRAIN DO?

Your brain is the control center of your body. It tells your legs when to move. It helps your hands open a door. It also tells your body to jump out of the way when a car is coming.

The brain is made up of special kinds of **cells** called nerve cells or neurons (NER-onz). Each neuron has tiny branches coming off of it. These branches link to other cells. Chemical messages travel from cell to cell through these links.

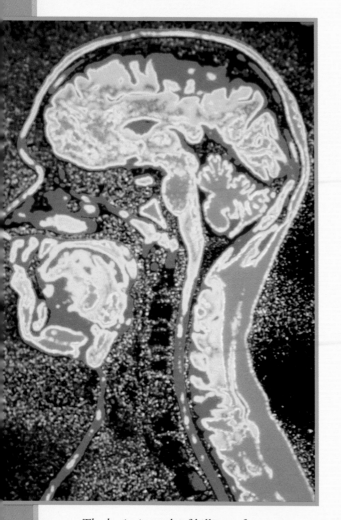

The brain is made of billions of neurons that control how you think, act, and feel.

The brain uses about 100 billion cells to do its job. These cells add up to almost 3 pounds (1.3 kilograms) of **tissue** in the head. Your brain did most of its growing when you were a baby. Still, every time you learn something new, your brain changes.

Doctors think that different parts of the brain have different jobs. Your feelings come from two small areas called the amygdala (ah-MIG-duh-luh). When you feel excited about going to a birthday party, you know that your amygdala is doing its job.

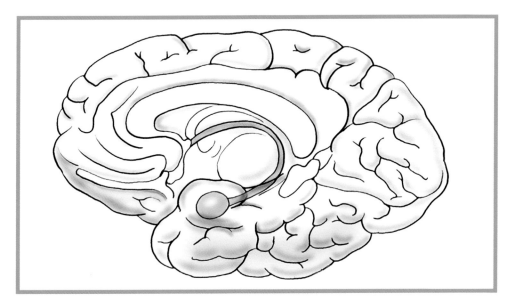

The amygdala, in red, is the part of your brain that controls your emotions.

Feeling excited or nervous can be a good thing. When this happens, your body makes **adrenaline.** Adrenaline gives your body and brain extra energy. It might be the boost you need to hit a home run.

Some people call this a "flight or fight" response. Early humans felt that boost of adrenaline when they faced large animals. It helped them decide if they should run away to safety or stay and fight.

Adrenaline gives your body a boost of energy when you need it most.

Learning how to handle emotions is part of growing up. Two-year-olds will cry and throw a tantrum when they get mad. They might hit or bite. But as they grow, their brains will change. They will learn that there are better ways to let someone know when they are angry.

Autism

Smiling, laughing, and being with friends are all normal parts of life for most of us. For children with autism, however, they are not. Autism is a disorder of the brain. Children with autism do not understand feelings the way other children do. They may have trouble knowing that a smile means someone is happy. Learning to talk and understand others is hard, too.

Doctors think autism happens when some of the neurons in the brain do not grow as large as they should. You may know someone at school with autism. If so, never tease or make fun of the student. Remember that people with autism may just experience the world differently from the way you do. Be a good friend.

CHAPTER THREE

DOES WORRYING HELP?

Has this ever happened to you? The teacher assigns a book report. You will have to write about the book you read. Then you will have to stand up in front of the class and talk about it. Your best friend is worried. Writing is easy for her, but talking in front of the class is scary.

Different people get nervous about different things. Writing is easy for your friend but hard for you. Public speaking is fun for you, but it makes your friend nervous.

You think talking to the class will be fun. But you dread writing the report. You are worried that your report won't be as good as everyone else's.

When you worry, you are feeling anxiety (ang-ZYE-ah-tee). Sometimes a little bit of worry is good. It

Worrying too much can prevent you from doing the things you need to do and from having fun.

can make you work harder. But worrying too much can keep you from doing your best.

There are many things you can do to help control your anxiety. Say you are worried about catching the ball during a softball game.

Practice will help your brain react better when it comes time to make an important play.

First, tell yourself that you can do it. Think about the times when you have caught it. Do not tell yourself that you will miss the ball.

You could also practice catching, maybe with a friend or an adult. This will help you develop the skills you need. Doing it over and over again helps your brain learn what to do in a game. Preparing yourself will make you feel more confident that you can make that important catch.

Before you run to the outfield, take a deep breath. That brings lots of oxygen to your brain. Oxygen helps your brain do its job. It will also help you calm down and be focused on what you need to do.

You might practice hard and still not be good at catching. You just might not enjoy playing softball. That is okay, too. Think about taking a break from being on the team. In another year or two, you might be ready to try softball again.

When you are worried about something, talk to a teacher or parent. Sometimes it helps just to let someone know how you are feeling. They can help you deal with your feelings. Then you can feel good about yourself.

Talking to a teacher about your worries can help you feel better about yourself.

CHAPTER FOUR

WHAT IS STRESS?

"What a bad day! I had too much stress at work!" You might hear

your parents say that at night when they come home. You might

feel the same way after a big test at school.

Each day, you face different kinds

of pressure. For example, getting your

work done quickly so you can go

*Taking a test or trying out for your school band
are pressures that might make you feel stress.*

Most stress does not last for long. As soon as the test is over or you get it back, you will feel better again.

outside to play is one type of pressure. Trying out for the school band is another. The feeling you have about these pressures is called stress.

Most stress lasts for a short period of time. Your stress about a test ends after you get your graded paper back. It is just a normal part of the day.

Some events cause stress that lasts for weeks or months. Some people feel this when a parent or grandparent is in the hospital. It is

Stress can sometimes make friends act strangely. They might want to be alone or with family instead of with you.

also a common feeling if you move to a new city or to a new school.

When stress lasts for a long time, people's be-havior might change. You might notice this in friends whose parents get a divorce. Your best friend might not want to spend the night at your house for a while. Being with a parent may be more important to your friend than being with you.

Adults can help children learn to handle stress like this. You can help, too. Do not make fun of your friends when they are dealing with stress. Try not to let their new behavior hurt your feelings, either. Let them know that you are still their friend. After a while, you and your friend will enjoy being with each other again.

The attacks on New York City and Washington, D.C., on September 11, 2001, added to the stress of many people. Watching the news reports on TV caused some children to worry. They

Let your friend know that you are still their friend.
That is the most important thing for them.

Talk to a parent or another adult if you are feeling too much stress.

wondered if what they saw on TV could happen to them. They did not feel safe. Remember that news reports are made for adults. Be sure an adult is with you if you watch them. Ask questions if you see something that upsets you.

How do you know if you are feeling too much stress? You might cry or get angry when simple things go wrong. Your head or stomach might hurt. If this happens to you, talk to an adult. A parent or teacher can help you learn to deal with feelings of stress. Then you will feel like your old self again!

CHAPTER FIVE

How Can You Develop Good Mental Health?

You can help your brain handle your emotions. That is part

of developing good mental health. Many of the things that

make your heart and muscles healthy will also help your brain.

*Activities that are good for your body are also good for
your mental health, such as running outdoors.*

First, make sure you get plenty of sleep each night. Scientists

think that the brain stores new information when you are asleep.

Sleep helps you think and remember things the next day.

Getting enough sleep each night helps you feel your best.

*If you get enough sleep during the night,
you should wake up feeling rested.
If not, you may feel cranky.*

Most children need about nine

hours of sleep. You should wake up

easily in the morning if you have had enough sleep. Lack of sleep

may put you in a bad mood. Then you will feel cranky when

things do not go right.

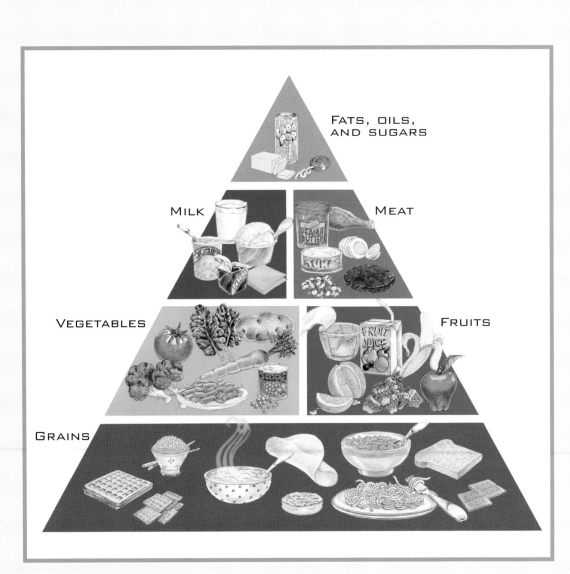

FATS, OILS, AND SUGARS

MILK

MEAT

VEGETABLES

FRUITS

GRAINS

Get to know the Food Pyramid Guide to help you make good food choices.

Next, make sure you are eating healthy foods. What you eat and

how much you eat can affect how you feel about the day. Learning

about the Food Guide Pyramid can help you make good food choices.

You should eat more of the foods at the bottom of the food pyramid than at the top. At the bottom are foods such as whole-grain bread, rice, vegetables, and fruit. At the top are things such as candy, cake, and cookies. You do not need to eat many of these each day.

Eating healthy foods keeps you feeling good.

Another way to reduce stress or anxiety is to have hobbies.

Playing or listening to music can be very soothing. Painting or

drawing a picture for your mom or dad or sister is another way

to relax. Working on a stamp or coin collection might also help.

Hobbies such as painting can let you relax and express yourself.

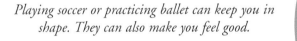

Playing soccer or practicing ballet can keep you in shape. They can also make you feel good.

Staying active can help all

children. When you exercise, your

lungs take in lots of oxygen. Then your heart

beats harder to send the oxygen to your muscles. The oxygen goes

to your brain, too.

Sometimes exercise will help your mood. Maybe you had

a day where everything went wrong. You spilled your milk at

breakfast. You forgot your homework. Your best friend is angry

with you. You feel lousy.

Try exercise to make yourself feel better. Turn on some music

and dance. Go shoot some hoops. Put on your helmet and ride

your bike. When you exercise, your body releases chemicals called

If you are upset or sad, try getting some exercise with a friend.
Sometimes that's just what you need to feel better.

endorphins (en-DOOR-fins). These help your brain make you feel happy.

Every day, you will experience lots of different feelings. You might be sad, happy, and excited all in the same day. That is normal. It also keeps every day from being the same. How did you feel today?

It's Hard to Sit Still!

Do you know anybody who has Attention Deficit Hyper-activity Disorder, or ADHD? If so, you know that your friend has a busy mind and a busy body.

Children and adults who have ADHD often have trouble keeping their minds focused on one project at a time. In class, students with ADHD may have trouble listening to the teacher or finishing their work. Getting up and walking around the room might be more interesting.

Doctors think that certain parts of the brain work differently in people with ADHD. Their brains are healthy, so they can do everything that people without ADHD can do. They just might need help from their friends and teachers to stay focused and do their best.

Glossary

adrenaline (uh-DRE-nuh-lin) Adrenaline is a hormone that gives the body a burst of energy.

cells (SEHLZ) A cell is the smallest living part of an organism.

mental (MEN-tuhl) Something that is mental has to do with the mind.

tissue (TISH-yoo) Tissue is a group of cells that forms part of the body.

Questions and Answers about Mental Health

What is a child psychiatrist? A child psychiatrist is a medical doctor who can identify and treat mental health problems affecting children, teens, and their families.

What is the best way to handle a bully? Walk away or tell the bully to leave you alone. Stick with a group of friends. A bully usually does not pick on children who are with others. If the bullying continues, tell an adult.

What is a phobia? A phobia is the fear of something specific, like a fear of spiders, a fear of heights, or a fear of flying in an airplane.

Is it okay to cry? People cry for many reasons. Often, we cry when we are sad, but sometimes we cry when we are happy, frustrated, or excited. Crying can be good because it can make you feel better. If you find yourself crying over little things or crying all the time, you should talk to an adult.

Did You Know?

‣ *Amygdala* is a Latin word that means "almond." The amygdala in the brain is shaped like an almond.

‣ About one out of every 20 people has Attention Deficit Hyperactivity Disorder.

‣ Having pets can help children feel good about themselves. Children who help take care of their pets develop self-confidence and learn about friendship.

‣ About 5 percent of children and teens suffer from depression. Common signs of depression include feeling hopeless, crying easily, and losing interest in activities.

‣ Each year, almost one million children have injuries to their brains. These injuries may be mild or severe. Brain injury is the leading cause of death in bike accidents. Wearing a helmet can help protect the brain from injury.

Being prepared for a test and doing well can make you feel very happy.

How to Learn More about Mental Health

At the Library: Fiction
Brown, Laurene Krasny, and Marc Brown. *Dinosaurs Divorce.*
Boston: Atlantic Monthly Press, 1986.
Viorst, Judith. *Alexander and the Terrible, Horrible, No Good, Very Bad Day.*
New York: Atheneum, 1972.

At the Library: Nonfiction
Crary, Elizabeth, and Jean Whitney (illustrator). *I'm Mad.*
Seattle: Parenting Press, 1992.

Perry, Susan, and Anastasia Mitchell (illustrator). *How Are You Feeling Today?*
Chanhassen, Minn.: The Child's World, 1993.

Wilde, Jerry. *Hot Stuff to Help Kids Chill Out.*
East Troy, Wis.: Lgr Productions, 1997.

Williams, Mary L., and Dianne O'Quinn Burke (illustrator). *Cool Cats, Calm Kids: Relaxation and Stress Management for Young People.* San Luis Obispo, Calif.: Impact Publishers, Inc., 1996.

On the Web
Visit our home page for lots of links about good mental health:
http://www.childsworld.com/links.html

Note to Parents, Teachers, and Librarians: We routinely verify our
Web links to make sure they're safe, active sites—so encourage your
readers to check them out!

Through the Mail or by Phone
Center for Mental Health Services
P.O. Box 42490
Washington, DC 20015
800/789-2647

National Mental Health Association
2001 North Beauregard Street, 12th Floor
Alexandria, VA 22311
800/969-6642

National Institute of Mental Health
6001 Executive Boulevard
Room 8184, MSC 9663
Bethesda, MD 20892-9663
301/443-4513

Friends make even tough days so much easier!

Index

adrenaline, 8
amygdala, 7
anger, 9, 18, 21
anxiety, 11–12, 24
Attention Deficit Hyperactivity Disorder
    (ADHD), 27
autism, 9

brain, 5, 6–7, 9, 12, 19, 25, 27

cells, 6–7, 9

emotions, 5, 7, 9, 19
endorphins, 27
excitement, 5, 7–8
exercise, 25–27

feelings. See emotions.
"flight or fight" response, 8
Food Guide Pyramid, 22–23
foods, 22–23

heart, 19, 25
hobbies, 24

lungs, 25

muscles, 19, 25

nerve cells. See neurons.
nervousness, 5, 8
neurons, 6–7, 9
news reports, 17–18

oxygen, 12–13, 25

September 11 attacks, 17–18
sleep, 20–21
stress, 14, 15–18, 24

tantrums, 9

worry. See anxiety.

About the Author

Shirley Wimbish Gray has been a writer and educator for more than 25 years and has published more than a dozen nonfiction books for children. She also coordinates cancer education programs at the University of Arkansas for Medical Sciences and consults as a writer with scientists and physicians. She lives with her husband and two sons in Little Rock, Arkansas.